A brighter tomorrow is a consequence of a purposeful today.

SAM PENNY
The Topify Method

topifymethod.com

Chips Investments Pty Ltd
Parcel Collect 10042 76215
Shop 4, 44 Landsborough Parade
Golden Beach QLD 4551 Australia

Chips
Investments
AUST

Chips Investments Pty Ltd is the publisher of this book. More information can be found at www.topifymethod.com.

Copyright © Sam Penny 2025

All rights reserved. No part of this book may be reproduced, stored in a retrieval system, or transmitted in any form or by any means—electronic, mechanical, photocopying, recording, or otherwise—without prior written permission from the publisher, except for brief quotations used in a review or critical analysis.

A CIP catalogue record for this book is available from the National Library of Australia.
ISBN 978-1-7638968-1-9

Design by Sam Penny

Chips Investments Pty Ltd is committed to sustainability. This book is printed on paper sourced from responsibly managed forests.

DEDICATION

For all the doers out there. Go forth an conquer.

How to Use The Topify Method

Welcome to The Topify Method, your simple and effective tool for staying focused and making progress every day. This journal is designed for everyone—mums, business owners, travellers, artists—anyone looking to make the most of their time and achieve more.

At the heart of this planner is The Topify Method—a simple yet powerful system to help you align your daily actions with your bigger goals. Each Quarter, Month, Week, and Day, you'll write down your Top 5 priorities and focus on completing at least the Top 1. Small steps, taken consistently, lead to big results.

Celebrate each achievement!

SCAN TO LEARN MORE

How to Achieve More

Quarterly Focus
Write down your Top 3 Priorities for the next three months. These will guide your monthly and weekly plans to ensure every step moves you forward.

Monthly Focus
From your quarterly goals, choose the Top 5 things to accomplish this month. Keep it clear and actionable.

Weekly Focus
Break your monthly goals into smaller actions. Write down the Top 5 tasks for the week and focus on making progress.

Daily Focus
Each day, list your Top 5 tasks and commit to completing at least the Top 1. Progress comes from action.

Reflection & Looking Ahead
Take a moment at the end of each period—whether it's a day, week, month, or quarter—to reflect on your progress. What worked well? What challenges did you overcome? Celebrate your achievements, no matter how small. Then, look ahead—what's the next step to keep moving forward?

This planner is here to simplify your productivity, keep you focused, and help you achieve more—one step at a time. Let's make every day count!

SCAN TO LEARN MORE

Quarter: _____ to _____

My 3 Big Priorities This Quarter

Priority 1:

Priority 2:

Priority 3:

Why these 3?

Priority 1:

Priority 2:

Priority 3:

What Does Success Look Like?

Priority 1: _____

_____

Priority 2: _____

_____

Priority 3: _____

_____

My Top 5 for Alignment

Main Focus: _____

Consistent Action: _____

Quick Wins: _____

_____

_____

Biggest Challenge: _____

One Rule to Follow: _____

Quarterly Commitment Statement

I commit to _____ over the next 90 days because _____

_____

_____

Month: _____

My Top 5 for this Month

Top 1 Done
◯ ☐ _____

◯ ☐ _____

◯ ☐ _____

◯ ☐ _____

◯ ☐ _____

Are these aligned with my Quarterly Top 5?

Energy flows, where focus goes.

Week Starting: _____

My Top 5 for this Week

Top 1 Done

○ ☐ _____

○ ☐ _____

○ ☐ _____

○ ☐ _____

○ ☐ _____

Are these aligned with my Monthly Top 5?

Your future self is watching - go!

My top 5 for today

Top 1 Done

◯ ☐ _____

◯ ☐ _____

◯ ☐ _____

◯ ☐ _____

◯ ☐ _____

Are these aligned with my Weekly Top 5?

A little progress daily overshadows a lifetime of perfect planning.

Date: _____ Day: _____ (1)

My top win today was:

Today I am grateful for:

My top 5 for today

Top 1 Done

○ ☐ _____

○ ☐ _____

○ ☐ _____

○ ☐ _____

○ ☐ _____

Are these aligned with my Weekly Top 5?

Remember to honor your growth, even when it feels slow.

Date: _____ Day: _____   (2)

My top win today was: _____

Today I am grateful for: _____

My top 5 for today

Top 1 Done

○ ☐ _____

○ ☐ _____

○ ☐ _____

○ ☐ _____

○ ☐ _____

Are these aligned with my Weekly Top 5?

Gratitude is an inner compass pointing you toward joy.

Date: _____ Day: _____ ③

My top win today was:

Today I am grateful for:

My top 5 for today

Top 1 Done

○ □ _____

○ □ _____

○ □ _____

○ □ _____

○ □ _____

Are these aligned with my Weekly Top 5?

Invest time in actions that move you forward, not in clock-watching.

Date: _____ Day: _____ (4)

My top win today was: _____

Today I am grateful for: _____

My top 5 for today

Top 1 Done

○ ☐ _____

○ ☐ _____

○ ☐ _____

○ ☐ _____

○ ☐ _____

Are these aligned with my Weekly Top 5?

Ready or not, your aspirations are calling—answer now.

Date: _____ Day: _____   (5)

My top win today was: _____

Today I am grateful for: _____

My top 5 for today

Top 1   Done

○ ☐ _____

○ ☐ _____

○ ☐ _____

○ ☐ _____

○ ☐ _____

Are these aligned with my Weekly Top 5?

Let your scars tell a story of self-rescue, not self-pity.

Date: _____ Day: _____ (6)

My top win today was:

Today I am grateful for:

My top 5 for today

Top 1 Done

○ ☐ _____

○ ☐ _____

○ ☐ _____

○ ☐ _____

○ ☐ _____

Are these aligned with my Weekly Top 5?

A grateful spirit invites success, while a critical one chases it away.

Date: _____ Day: _____ (7)

My top win today was: _____

Today I am grateful for: _____

Week Ending: _____

①

My Week in Review

My top win this week was:

I am grateful for:

What could be improved or learned:

Week Starting: _____   (2)

My Top 5 for this Week

Top 1 Done

○ ☐ _____

○ ☐ _____

○ ☐ _____

○ ☐ _____

○ ☐ _____

Are these aligned with my Monthly Top 5?

Done is better than perfect.

My top 5 for today

Top 1 Done

○ ☐ _____

○ ☐ _____

○ ☐ _____

○ ☐ _____

○ ☐ _____

Are these aligned with my Weekly Top 5?

Recalibrate your life by tending carefully to the now.

Date: Day: (8)

My top win today was:

Today I am grateful for:

My top 5 for today

Top 1 Done

○ ☐ _____

○ ☐ _____

○ ☐ _____

○ ☐ _____

○ ☐ _____

Are these aligned with my Weekly Top 5?

Prove to yourself you can do it; nobody else's opinion matters anyway.

Date: _____ Day: _____ (9)

My top win today was: _____

Today I am grateful for: _____

My top 5 for today

Top 1   Done

◯ ☐ _____

◯ ☐ _____

◯ ☐ _____

◯ ☐ _____

◯ ☐ _____

Are these aligned with my Weekly Top 5?

Your potential waits on the other side of consistent effort.

Date: _____ Day: _____ (10)

My top win today was: _____

Today I am grateful for: _____

My top 5 for today

Top 1   Done

○ ☐ _____

○ ☐ _____

○ ☐ _____

○ ☐ _____

○ ☐ _____

Are these aligned with my Weekly Top 5?

Recognize the silver linings—they shine brighter under gratitude's light.

Date: _____ Day: _____ (11)

My top win today was: _____

Today I am grateful for: _____

My top 5 for today

Top 1 Done
○ ☐ _____

○ ☐ _____

○ ☐ _____

○ ☐ _____

○ ☐ _____

Are these aligned with my Weekly Top 5?

Don't wait for perfect to give yourself permission to begin.

Date: _____ Day: _____ (12)

My top win today was: _____

Today I am grateful for: _____

My top 5 for today

Top 1 Done

○ ☐ _____

○ ☐ _____

○ ☐ _____

○ ☐ _____

○ ☐ _____

Are these aligned with my Weekly Top 5?

Inspiration often follows action, not the other way around.

Date: _____ Day: _____ (13)

My top win today was: _____

Today I am grateful for: _____

My top 5 for today

Top 1 Done

○ ☐ _____

○ ☐ _____

○ ☐ _____

○ ☐ _____

○ ☐ _____

Are these aligned with my Weekly Top 5?

Recognizing simple gifts keeps your spirit open to greater ones.

Date: _____ Day: _____ (14)

My top win today was:

Today I am grateful for:

Week Ending: _____

My Week in Review

My top win this week was:

_____
_____
_____

I am grateful for:

_____
_____
_____

What could be improved or learned:

_____
_____
_____

Week Starting: _____ (3)

My Top 5 for this Week

Top 1 Done
○ ☐ _____

○ ☐ _____

○ ☐ _____

○ ☐ _____

○ ☐ _____

Are these aligned with my Monthly Top 5?

Small steps, big results.

My top 5 for today

Top 1 Done

○ □ _____

○ □ _____

○ □ _____

○ □ _____

○ □ _____

Are these aligned with my Weekly Top 5?

Meet your deadlines like they're promises to yourself.

Date: _____ Day: _____ (15)

My top win today was: _____

Today I am grateful for: _____

My top 5 for today

Top 1   Done

○ ☐

○ ☐

○ ☐

○ ☐

○ ☐

Are these aligned with my Weekly Top 5?

Imperfect effort always outvalues perfect inaction.

Date: _____ Day: _____ (16)

My top win today was: _____

Today I am grateful for: _____

My top 5 for today

Top 1 Done

○ ☐ _____

○ ☐ _____

○ ☐ _____

○ ☐ _____

○ ☐ _____

Are these aligned with my Weekly Top 5?

Recognizing what you have turns scarcity into plenty.

Date: _____ Day: _____ (17)

My top win today was: _____

Today I am grateful for: _____

My top 5 for today

Top 1 Done

○ ☐ _____

○ ☐ _____

○ ☐ _____

○ ☐ _____

○ ☐ _____

Are these aligned with my Weekly Top 5?

Your future thrives when you invest in your present wholeheartedly.

Date: Day:

(18)

My top win today was:

Today I am grateful for:

My top 5 for today

Top 1 Done

○ □ _____

○ □ _____

○ □ _____

○ □ _____

○ □ _____

Are these aligned with my Weekly Top 5?

Initiate action, and momentum will find you.

Date: _____ Day: _____ (19)

My top win today was: _____

Today I am grateful for: _____

My top 5 for today

Top 1 Done

◯ ☐ _____

◯ ☐ _____

◯ ☐ _____

◯ ☐ _____

◯ ☐ _____

Are these aligned with my Weekly Top 5?

Refine your methods, accelerate your results.

Date: _____ Day: _____ 20

My top win today was: _____

Today I am grateful for: _____

My top 5 for today

Top 1 Done

○ ☐ _____

○ ☐ _____

○ ☐ _____

○ ☐ _____

○ ☐ _____

Are these aligned with my Weekly Top 5?

Forge your future with today's focused work.

Date: Day:

(21)

My top win today was:

Today I am grateful for:

Week Ending: _____

My Week in Review

My top win this week was:

_____
_____
_____

I am grateful for:

_____
_____
_____

What could be improved or learned:

_____
_____

Week Starting: _____ (4)

My Top 5 for this Week

Top 1 Done
○ ☐ _____

○ ☐ _____

○ ☐ _____

○ ☐ _____

○ ☐ _____

Are these aligned with my Monthly Top 5?

One task. Full focus. Crush it.

My top 5 for today

Top 1 Done
○ ☐ _____

○ ☐ _____

○ ☐ _____

○ ☐ _____

○ ☐ _____

Are these aligned with my Weekly Top 5?

Your spark of enthusiasm must catch
fire through daily effort.

Date: _____ Day: _____ (22)

My top win today was: _____

Today I am grateful for: _____

My top 5 for today

Top 1 Done

○ ☐ _____

○ ☐ _____

○ ☐ _____

○ ☐ _____

○ ☐ _____

Are these aligned with my Weekly Top 5?

Refuse to be defeated by the silence—
your echo is all you need.

Date: _____ Day: _____ (23)

My top win today was:

Today I am grateful for:

My top 5 for today

Top 1 Done

○ ☐ _____

○ ☐ _____

○ ☐ _____

○ ☐ _____

○ ☐ _____

Are these aligned with my Weekly Top 5?

Offer yourself the kindness you freely give others.

Date: _____ Day: _____ (24)

My top win today was: _____

Today I am grateful for: _____

My top 5 for today

Top 1 Done

○ ☐ _____

○ ☐ _____

○ ☐ _____

○ ☐ _____

○ ☐ _____

Are these aligned with my Weekly Top 5?

Your success isn't up for a popular vote;
claim it whether they cheer or not.

Date: _____ Day: _____ (25)

My top win today was: _____

Today I am grateful for: _____

My top 5 for today

Top 1 Done
○ ☐ _____

○ ☐ _____

○ ☐ _____

○ ☐ _____

○ ☐ _____

Are these aligned with my Weekly Top 5?

Refuse to be minimized by people who can't see your full height.

Date: _____ Day: _____ (26)

My top win today was:

Today I am grateful for:

My top 5 for today

Top 1   Done

○ ☐ _____

○ ☐ _____

○ ☐ _____

○ ☐ _____

○ ☐ _____

Are these aligned with my Weekly Top 5?

Simplicity in the present paves the way
for clarity in the future.

Date: _____ Day: _____   (27)

My top win today was:

Today I am grateful for:

My top 5 for today

Top 1 Done

○ ☐ _____

○ ☐ _____

○ ☐ _____

○ ☐ _____

○ ☐ _____

Are these aligned with my Weekly Top 5?

Imperfections make you real; progress makes you unstoppable.

Date: _____ Day: _____ (28)

My top win today was: _____

Today I am grateful for: _____

Week Ending: _____

My Week in Review

My top win this week was:

_____
_____
_____

I am grateful for:

_____
_____
_____

What could be improved or learned:

_____
_____
_____

Week Starting: _____

(5)

My Top 5 for this Week

Top 1   Done

○ ☐ _____

○ ☐ _____

○ ☐ _____

○ ☐ _____

○ ☐ _____

Are these aligned with my Monthly Top 5?

Win the day, every day.

My top 5 for today

Top 1   Done

○ ☐ _____

○ ☐ _____

○ ☐ _____

○ ☐ _____

○ ☐ _____

Are these aligned with my Weekly Top 5?

Reject the urge to fit their mold; your uniqueness is a gift, not a flaw.

Date: Day: (29)

My top win today was:

Today I am grateful for:

My top 5 for today

Top 1 Done
○ ☐ _____

○ ☐ _____

○ ☐ _____

○ ☐ _____

○ ☐ _____

Are these aligned with my Weekly Top 5?

Each task you finish is a vote for the future you desire.

Date: Day: (30)

My top win today was:

Today I am grateful for:

My top 5 for today

Top 1 Done
○ ☐ _____

○ ☐ _____

○ ☐ _____

○ ☐ _____

○ ☐ _____

Are these aligned with my Weekly Top 5?

In productivity, small efforts create ripples of success.

Date: _____ Day: _____ (31)

My top win today was: _____

Today I am grateful for: _____

Month: _____

My Month in Review

My top win last month was:

_____
_____
_____

I am grateful for:

_____
_____
_____

What could be improved or learned:

_____
_____
_____

Month: _____

②

My Top 5 for this Month

Top 1 Done

○ ☐ _____

○ ☐ _____

○ ☐ _____

○ ☐ _____

○ ☐ _____

Are these aligned with my Quarterly Top 5?

Less thinking, more doing.

Week Ending: _____

My Week in Review

My top win this week was:

I am grateful for:

What could be improved or learned:

Week Starting: _____

My Top 5 for this Week

Top 1 Done
○ ☐ _____

○ ☐ _____

○ ☐ _____

○ ☐ _____

○ ☐ _____

Are these aligned with my Monthly Top 5?

Success loves speed.

My top 5 for today

Top 1 Done

○ ☐ _____

○ ☐ _____

○ ☐ _____

○ ☐ _____

○ ☐ _____

Are these aligned with my Weekly Top 5?

Real victory is thriving in a world that shows you no special favour.

Date: _____ Day: _____ (1)

My top win today was:

Today I am grateful for:

My top 5 for today

Top 1   Done

○ ☐ _____

○ ☐ _____

○ ☐ _____

○ ☐ _____

○ ☐ _____

Are these aligned with my Weekly Top 5?

Show up like your best self already exists—then become it.

Date: _____ Day: _____

My top win today was: _____

Today I am grateful for: _____

My top 5 for today

Top 1 Done

○ ☐ _____

○ ☐ _____

○ ☐ _____

○ ☐ _____

○ ☐ _____

Are these aligned with my Weekly Top 5?

Hustle early, celebrate later.

Date: Day: 3

My top win today was:

Today I am grateful for:

My top 5 for today

Top 1 Done

○ ☐ _____

○ ☐ _____

○ ☐ _____

○ ☐ _____

○ ☐ _____

Are these aligned with my Weekly Top 5?

Productivity grows best in the soil of consistency.

Date: _____   Day: _____   (4)

My top win today was: _____

Today I am grateful for: _____

My top 5 for today

Top 1   Done

○ ☐ _____

○ ☐ _____

○ ☐ _____

○ ☐ _____

○ ☐ _____

Are these aligned with my Weekly Top 5?

Shape the now, and the future will conform to your vision.

Date: _____   Day: _____   (5)

My top win today was:

Today I am grateful for:

My top 5 for today

Top 1 Done

○ ☐ _____

○ ☐ _____

○ ☐ _____

○ ☐ _____

○ ☐ _____

Are these aligned with my Weekly Top 5?

Action begets motivation, not the other way around.

Date: _____ Day: _____ ⑥

My top win today was: _____

Today I am grateful for: _____

My top 5 for today

Top 1 Done

○ ☐ _____

○ ☐ _____

○ ☐ _____

○ ☐ _____

○ ☐ _____

Are these aligned with my Weekly Top 5?

Simplicity is clarity in motion.

Date: _____ Day: _____ (7)

My top win today was: _____

Today I am grateful for: _____

Week Ending: _____

My Week in Review

My top win this week was:

_____
_____
_____

I am grateful for:

_____
_____
_____

What could be improved or learned:

_____
_____
_____

Week Starting: _____

My Top 5 for this Week

Top 1 Done

○ ☐ _____

○ ☐ _____

○ ☐ _____

○ ☐ _____

○ ☐ _____

Are these aligned with my Monthly Top 5?

Action beats intention - start now, refine later.

My top 5 for today

Top 1   Done
○ ☐ _____

○ ☐ _____

○ ☐ _____

○ ☐ _____

○ ☐ _____

Are these aligned with my Weekly Top 5?

See yourself as limitless; the universe is waiting for your brilliance.

Date: _____   Day: _____   (8)

My top win today was: _____

Today I am grateful for: _____

My top 5 for today

Top 1   Done

○ ☐ _____

○ ☐ _____

○ ☐ _____

○ ☐ _____

○ ☐ _____

Are these aligned with my Weekly Top 5?

Your best ally is progress, your worst enemy is perfect.

Date: _____ Day: _____   (9)

My top win today was: _____

Today I am grateful for: _____

My top 5 for today

Top 1 Done

○ ☐ _____

○ ☐ _____

○ ☐ _____

○ ☐ _____

○ ☐ _____

Are these aligned with my Weekly Top 5?

Simplicity sparks efficiency.

Date: _____   Day: _____   (10)

My top win today was:

Today I am grateful for:

My top 5 for today

Top 1 Done

○ ☐ _____

○ ☐ _____

○ ☐ _____

○ ☐ _____

○ ☐ _____

Are these aligned with my Weekly Top 5?

Say goodbye to hesitation; clock in to your future.

Date: Day: (11)

My top win today was:

Today I am grateful for:

My top 5 for today

Top 1   Done

○ □ _____

○ □ _____

○ □ _____

○ □ _____

○ □ _____

Are these aligned with my Weekly Top 5?

Action separates the dreamers from the doers.

Date: Day: (12)

My top win today was:

Today I am grateful for:

My top 5 for today

Top 1   Done
○ □ _____

○ □ _____

○ □ _____

○ □ _____

○ □ _____
Are these aligned with my Weekly Top 5?

Stay alert to the gift of the present; it holds the spark of transformation.

Date: _____ Day: _____   (13)

My top win today was:

Today I am grateful for:

My top 5 for today

Top 1 Done

○ ☐ _____

○ ☐ _____

○ ☐ _____

○ ☐ _____

○ ☐ _____

Are these aligned with my Weekly Top 5?

Say 'thank you' to your past—it helped you arrive where you stand today.

Date: _____   Day: _____   (14)

My top win today was: _____

Today I am grateful for: _____

Week Ending: _____

My Week in Review

My top win this week was:

_____
_____
_____

I am grateful for:

_____
_____
_____

What could be improved or learned:

_____
_____
_____

Week Starting: _____

⑧

My Top 5 for this Week

Top 1 Done

○ ☐ _____

○ ☐ _____

○ ☐ _____

○ ☐ _____

○ ☐ _____

Are these aligned with my Monthly Top 5?

Progress > Perfection - Just Start

My top 5 for today

Top 1 Done
○ ☐ _____

○ ☐ _____

○ ☐ _____

○ ☐ _____

○ ☐ _____

Are these aligned with my Weekly Top 5?

Gratitude gives wings to dreams and roots to success.

Date: Day: (15)

My top win today was:

Today I am grateful for:

My top 5 for today

Top 1   Done

○ ☐ _____

○ ☐ _____

○ ☐ _____

○ ☐ _____

○ ☐ _____

Are these aligned with my Weekly Top 5?

Step away from empty opinions and step into your higher potential.

Date: _____ Day: _____ (16)

My top win today was: _____

Today I am grateful for: _____

My top 5 for today

Top 1   Done

○ ☐ _____

○ ☐ _____

○ ☐ _____

○ ☐ _____

○ ☐ _____

Are these aligned with my Weekly Top 5?

A powerful future emerges when the present is handled with care.

Date: _____ Day: _____ (17)

My top win today was: _____

Today I am grateful for: _____

My top 5 for today

Top 1   Done

○ ☐ _____

○ ☐ _____

○ ☐ _____

○ ☐ _____

○ ☐ _____

Are these aligned with my Weekly Top 5?

Bold action is the quickest path to lasting motivation.

Date: _____ Day: _____ (18)

My top win today was: _____

Today I am grateful for: _____

My top 5 for today

Top 1   Done

○ ☐ _____

○ ☐ _____

○ ☐ _____

○ ☐ _____

○ ☐ _____

Are these aligned with my Weekly Top 5?

Step beyond your comfort zone;
perfection is a prison anyway.

Date: _____ Day: _____ (19)

My top win today was: _____

Today I am grateful for: _____

My top 5 for today

Top 1   Done
○ □ ....

○ □ ....

○ □ ....

○ □ ....

○ □ ....

Are these aligned with my Weekly Top 5?

Your future thrives on your resolve, not their approval.

Date: _____ Day: _____ (20)

My top win today was: _____

Today I am grateful for: _____

My top 5 for today

Top 1 Done
○ □ _____

○ □ _____

○ □ _____

○ □ _____

○ □ _____

Are these aligned with my Weekly Top 5?

Work in silence; let your success speak volumes.

Date: _____ Day: _____   (21)

My top win today was: _____

Today I am grateful for: _____

Week Ending: _____

My Week in Review

My top win this week was:

_____
_____
_____

I am grateful for:

_____
_____
_____

What could be improved or learned:

_____
_____
_____

Week Starting: _____ (9)

My Top 5 for this Week

Top 1 Done
○ □ _____

○ □ _____

○ □ _____

○ □ _____

○ □ _____

Are these aligned with my Monthly Top 5?

Progress beats perfection.
Take one step forward this week.

My top 5 for today

Top 1　Done

○ ☐ _____

○ ☐ _____

○ ☐ _____

○ ☐ _____

○ ☐ _____

Are these aligned with my Weekly Top 5?

Stop aiming for perfect and start aiming for done.

Date: _____ Day: _____ (22)

My top win today was: _____

Today I am grateful for: _____

My top 5 for today

Top 1   Done
○ □ _____

○ □ _____

○ □ _____

○ □ _____

○ □ _____

Are these aligned with my Weekly Top 5?

A mindful approach to the present
expands every aspect of your future.

Date: _____ Day: _____ (23)

My top win today was: _____

Today I am grateful for: _____

My top 5 for today

Top 1 Done
○ □ _____

○ □ _____

○ □ _____

○ □ _____

○ □ _____

Are these aligned with my Weekly Top 5?

Big talk means nothing without the backbone of action.

Date: _____ Day: _____ (24)

My top win today was: _____

Today I am grateful for: _____

My top 5 for today

Top 1 Done
◯ ☐ _____

◯ ☐ _____

◯ ☐ _____

◯ ☐ _____

◯ ☐ _____

Are these aligned with my Weekly Top 5?

Stop chasing flawless; start chasing forward.

Date: Day: (25)

My top win today was:

Today I am grateful for:

My top 5 for today

Top 1   Done

○ ☐ _____

○ ☐ _____

○ ☐ _____

○ ☐ _____

○ ☐ _____

Are these aligned with my Weekly Top 5?

A kind thought toward yourself can change the entire day.

Date: _____ Day: _____ (26)

My top win today was: _____

Today I am grateful for: _____

My top 5 for today

Top 1   Done

○ ☐ _____

○ ☐ _____

○ ☐ _____

○ ☐ _____

○ ☐ _____

Are these aligned with my Weekly Top 5?

You are not invisible to yourself—take bold action that validates your existence.

Date: _____ Day: _____ (27)

My top win today was: _____

Today I am grateful for: _____

My top 5 for today

Top 1   Done

○ ☐ _____

○ ☐ _____

○ ☐ _____

○ ☐ _____

○ ☐ _____

Are these aligned with my Weekly Top 5?

Stop cramming your day with busywork; reserve space for real work.

Date: Day: (28)

My top win today was:

Today I am grateful for:

Week Ending: _____

My Week in Review

My top win this week was:

_____
_____
_____

I am grateful for:

_____
_____
_____

What could be improved or learned:

_____
_____
_____

Week Starting: _____

My Top 5 for this Week

Top 1 Done
○ ☐ _____

○ ☐ _____

○ ☐ _____

○ ☐ _____

○ ☐ _____

Are these aligned with my Monthly Top 5?

Perfection is a thief. Progress is the real prize.

My top 5 for today

Top 1 Done

○ ☐ _____

○ ☐ _____

○ ☐ _____

○ ☐ _____

○ ☐ _____

Are these aligned with my Weekly Top 5?

It's easy to feel worthless if you measure yourself by their lack of care—measure by your own grit instead.

Date: _____ Day: _____ (29)

My top win today was: _____

Today I am grateful for: _____

My top 5 for today

Top 1 Done

○ ☐ _____

○ ☐ _____

○ ☐ _____

○ ☐ _____

○ ☐ _____

Are these aligned with my Weekly Top 5?

Let your success speak for itself in a language only you need to hear.

Date: Day: (30)

My top win today was:

Today I am grateful for:

My top 5 for today

Top 1 Done

○ ☐ _____

○ ☐ _____

○ ☐ _____

○ ☐ _____

○ ☐ _____

Are these aligned with my Weekly Top 5?

Stop delaying; start delivering your greatness.

Date: _____ Day: _____ (31)

My top win today was: _____

Today I am grateful for: _____

Month: _____

My Month in Review

My top win last month was:
_____
_____
_____

I am grateful for:
_____
_____
_____

What could be improved or learned:
_____
_____
_____

Month: _____

③

My Top 5 for this Month

Top 1   Done

○ ☐ _____

○ ☐ _____

○ ☐ _____

○ ☐ _____

○ ☐ _____

Are these aligned with my Quarterly Top 5?

*Chasing perfection steals your time—
progress pays the real rewards.*

Week Ending: _____

(10)

My Week in Review

My top win this week was:

_____
_____
_____

I am grateful for:

_____
_____
_____

What could be improved or learned:

_____
_____
_____

Week Starting: _____

My Top 5 for this Week

Top 1   Done

○ ☐ _____

○ ☐ _____

○ ☐ _____

○ ☐ _____

○ ☐ _____

Are these aligned with my Monthly Top 5?

Perfection steals momentum. Progress builds success.

My top 5 for today

Top 1　Done

○ □ _____

○ □ _____

○ □ _____

○ □ _____

○ □ _____

Are these aligned with my Weekly Top 5?

Unlock your greatness by daring to believe in yourself.

Date: _____   Day: _____   (1)

My top win today was: _____

Today I am grateful for: _____

My top 5 for today

Top 1 Done

○ ☐ _____

○ ☐ _____

○ ☐ _____

○ ☐ _____

○ ☐ _____

Are these aligned with my Weekly Top 5?

Be ruthless with time wasters, generous with effort.

Date: _____   Day: _____   (2)

My top win today was: _____

Today I am grateful for: _____

My top 5 for today

Top 1 Done

○ □ _____

○ □ _____

○ □ _____

○ □ _____

○ □ _____

Are these aligned with my Weekly Top 5?

Stop dreaming your life—start living your dreams.

Date: _____ Day: _____ (3)

My top win today was: _____

Today I am grateful for: _____

My top 5 for today

Top 1 Done

○ ☐ _____

○ ☐ _____

○ ☐ _____

○ ☐ _____

○ ☐ _____

Are these aligned with my Weekly Top 5?

Invest in what matters most today, and your future will yield dividends of joy.

Date: _____ Day: _____ (4)

My top win today was: _____

Today I am grateful for: _____

My top 5 for today

Top 1   Done
○ ☐ _____

○ ☐ _____

○ ☐ _____

○ ☐ _____

○ ☐ _____

Are these aligned with my Weekly Top 5?

You can't refine what you never begin—
progress is the first move.

Date: _____ Day: _____ (5)

My top win today was: _____

Today I am grateful for: _____

My top 5 for today

Top 1 Done

○ ☐ _____

○ ☐ _____

○ ☐ _____

○ ☐ _____

○ ☐ _____

Are these aligned with my Weekly Top 5?

Start with grit, end with glory—keep the cycle going.

Date: _____ Day: _____ (6)

My top win today was: _____

Today I am grateful for: _____

My top 5 for today

Top 1 Done
○ ☐ _____

○ ☐ _____

○ ☐ _____

○ ☐ _____

○ ☐ _____

Are these aligned with my Weekly Top 5?

Your schedule reflects your seriousness.

Date: _____ Day: _____ (7)

My top win today was: _____

Today I am grateful for: _____

Week Ending: _____

My Week in Review

My top win this week was:

_____
_____
_____

I am grateful for:

_____
_____
_____

What could be improved or learned:

_____
_____
_____

Week Starting: _____

My Top 5 for this Week

Top 1 Done
○ ☐ _____

○ ☐ _____

○ ☐ _____

○ ☐ _____

○ ☐ _____

Are these aligned with my Monthly Top 5?

Own the week—start strong, finish stronger.

My top 5 for today

Top 1 Done

○ ☐ _____

○ ☐ _____

○ ☐ _____

○ ☐ _____

○ ☐ _____

Are these aligned with my Weekly Top 5?

Be grateful for progress, not just perfection.

Date: Day: (8)

My top win today was:

Today I am grateful for:

My top 5 for today

Top 1   Done

○ ☐ _____

○ ☐ _____

○ ☐ _____

○ ☐ _____

○ ☐ _____

Are these aligned with my Weekly Top 5?

Stop explaining your plan and start exploring your capabilities.

Date: _____   Day: _____   (9)

My top win today was: _____

Today I am grateful for: _____

My top 5 for today

Top 1   Done

○ ☐ _____

○ ☐ _____

○ ☐ _____

○ ☐ _____

○ ☐ _____

Are these aligned with my Weekly Top 5?

Your self-love story is the best bestseller you'll ever write.

Date: _____ Day: _____ (10)

My top win today was: _____

Today I am grateful for: _____

My top 5 for today

Top 1   Done

○ □ _____

○ □ _____

○ □ _____

○ □ _____

○ □ _____

Are these aligned with my Weekly Top 5?

You can't win if you don't begin—throw yourself into action.

Date: Day: (11)

My top win today was:

Today I am grateful for:

My top 5 for today

Top 1　Done

○ ☐ _____

○ ☐ _____

○ ☐ _____

○ ☐ _____

○ ☐ _____

Are these aligned with my Weekly Top 5?

Stop snoozing on your dreams—rise and make them real.

Date: _____   Day: _____   (12)

My top win today was: _____

Today I am grateful for: _____

My top 5 for today

Top 1   Done

○ ☐ _____

○ ☐ _____

○ ☐ _____

○ ☐ _____

○ ☐ _____

Are these aligned with my Weekly Top 5?

Prove to yourself that even without them, you're still unstoppable.

Date: _____ Day: _____ (13)

My top win today was: _____

Today I am grateful for: _____

My top 5 for today

Top 1   Done

○ ☐ _____

○ ☐ _____

○ ☐ _____

○ ☐ _____

○ ☐ _____

Are these aligned with my Weekly Top 5?

Great results come from tiny relentless efforts.

Date: Day: (14)

My top win today was:

Today I am grateful for:

Week Ending: _____

My Week in Review

My top win this week was:

_____
_____
_____

I am grateful for:

_____
_____
_____

What could be improved or learned:

_____
_____
_____

Week Starting: _____   (13)

My Top 5 for this Week

Top 1 Done
○ ☐ _____

○ ☐ _____

○ ☐ _____

○ ☐ _____

○ ☐ _____

Are these aligned with my Monthly Top 5?

Every day is a step forward—stack them wisely.

My top 5 for today

Top 1 Done

○ ☐ _____

○ ☐ _____

○ ☐ _____

○ ☐ _____

○ ☐ _____

Are these aligned with my Weekly Top 5?

Stop storing ideas in your head; set them free on paper.

Date: _____   Day: _____   (15)

My top win today was: _____

Today I am grateful for: _____

My top 5 for today

Top 1 Done

○ ☐ _____

○ ☐ _____

○ ☐ _____

○ ☐ _____

○ ☐ _____

Are these aligned with my Weekly Top 5?

Waiting for a spark? Light the match yourself.

Date: Day: (16)

My top win today was:

Today I am grateful for:

My top 5 for today

Top 1   Done

○ ☐ _____

○ ☐ _____

○ ☐ _____

○ ☐ _____

○ ☐ _____

Are these aligned with my Weekly Top 5?

Busy is a smoke screen; real success is built on tangible action.

Date: Day:

(17)

My top win today was:

Today I am grateful for:

My top 5 for today

Top 1   Done

○ ☐ _____

○ ☐ _____

○ ☐ _____

○ ☐ _____

○ ☐ _____

Are these aligned with my Weekly Top 5?

Stop waiting for support—build a foundation strong enough to hold your own ambitions.

Date: _____   Day: _____   (18)

My top win today was: _____

Today I am grateful for: _____

My top 5 for today

Top 1   Done

○ ☐ _____

○ ☐ _____

○ ☐ _____

○ ☐ _____

○ ☐ _____

Are these aligned with my Weekly Top 5?

A future of promise begins with an unwavering present.

Date: Day: (19)

My top win today was:

Today I am grateful for:

My top 5 for today

Top 1 Done

○ ☐ _____

○ ☐ _____

○ ☐ _____

○ ☐ _____

○ ☐ _____

Are these aligned with my Weekly Top 5?

Let your hustle talk louder than your words.

Date: _____ Day: _____ (20)

My top win today was: _____

Today I am grateful for: _____

My top 5 for today

Top 1 Done

○ ☐ _____

○ ☐ _____

○ ☐ _____

○ ☐ _____

○ ☐ _____

Are these aligned with my Weekly Top 5?

Stop waiting, start creating tangible results.

Date: Day: (21)

My top win today was:

Today I am grateful for:

Week Ending: _____

My Week in Review

My top win this week was:

_____
_____
_____

I am grateful for:

_____
_____
_____

What could be improved or learned:

_____
_____
_____

Week Starting: _____ (14)

My Top 5 for this Week

Top 1 Done

○ ☐ _____

○ ☐ _____

○ ☐ _____

○ ☐ _____

○ ☐ _____

Are these aligned with my Monthly Top 5?

Win the morning, win the week.

My top 5 for today

Top 1 Done
○ ☐ _____

○ ☐ _____

○ ☐ _____

○ ☐ _____

○ ☐ _____

Are these aligned with my Weekly Top 5?

In a room full of people who don't care,
choose to care about yourself.

Date: _____ Day: _____ (22)

My top win today was: _____

Today I am grateful for: _____

My top 5 for today

Top 1 Done
○ ☐ _____

○ ☐ _____

○ ☐ _____

○ ☐ _____

○ ☐ _____

Are these aligned with my Weekly Top 5?

You hold the power to transform this very moment into progress.

Date: _____ Day: _____ (23)

My top win today was: _____

Today I am grateful for: _____

My top 5 for today

Top 1 Done
○ ☐ _____

○ ☐ _____

○ ☐ _____

○ ☐ _____

○ ☐ _____

Are these aligned with my Weekly Top 5?

Store your tasks on paper, so your mind stays free to innovate.

Date: Day: (24)

My top win today was:

Today I am grateful for:

My top 5 for today

Top 1 Done

○ ☐ _____

○ ☐ _____

○ ☐ _____

○ ☐ _____

○ ☐ _____

Are these aligned with my Weekly Top 5?

Your tomorrow is shaped by how you treat yourself today.

Date: _____ Day: _____ (25)

My top win today was: _____

Today I am grateful for: _____

My top 5 for today

Top 1   Done

○ ☐ _____

○ ☐ _____

○ ☐ _____

○ ☐ _____

○ ☐ _____

Are these aligned with my Weekly Top 5?

Momentum is built on action, not intention.

Date: Day: 26

My top win today was:

Today I am grateful for:

My top 5 for today

Top 1 Done

○ ☐ _____

○ ☐ _____

○ ☐ _____

○ ☐ _____

○ ☐ _____

Are these aligned with my Weekly Top 5?

Strategic planning saves energy, but
only if you turn plans into deeds.

Date: Day:

27

My top win today was:

Today I am grateful for:

My top 5 for today

Top 1 Done
○ ☐ _____

○ ☐ _____

○ ☐ _____

○ ☐ _____

○ ☐ _____

Are these aligned with my Weekly Top 5?

Empty praise can't build you up; real strength comes from self-foundation.

Date: _____ Day: _____ (28)

My top win today was:

Today I am grateful for:

Week Ending: _____ (14)

My Week in Review

My top win this week was:

_____
_____
_____

I am grateful for:

_____
_____
_____

What could be improved or learned:

_____
_____
_____

Week Starting: _____ (15)

My Top 5 for this Week

Top 1 Done

○ ☐ _____

○ ☐ _____

○ ☐ _____

○ ☐ _____

○ ☐ _____

Are these aligned with my Monthly Top 5?

A productive week starts with a single focused task.

My top 5 for today

Top 1 Done

○ ☐ _____

○ ☐ _____

○ ☐ _____

○ ☐ _____

○ ☐ _____

Are these aligned with my Weekly Top 5?

Apathy is your sign to push harder, not to quit.

Date: Day: (29)

My top win today was:

Today I am grateful for:

My top 5 for today

Top 1 Done

○ ☐ _____

○ ☐ _____

○ ☐ _____

○ ☐ _____

○ ☐ _____

Are these aligned with my Weekly Top 5?

Strike while your motivation is hot—
don't let it fade.

Date: _____ Day: _____ (30)

My top win today was: _____

Today I am grateful for: _____

My top 5 for today

Top 1   Done

○ ☐ ....

○ ☐ ....

○ ☐ ....

○ ☐ ....

○ ☐ ....

Are these aligned with my Weekly Top 5?

Pour love into yourself so you can overflow it to others.

Date: _____ Day: _____ (31)

My top win today was: _____

Today I am grateful for: _____

Quarter: _____ to _____

My 3 Big Priorities This Quarter

Priority 1:
_____
_____

Priority 2:
_____
_____

Priority 3:
_____
_____

How Did I Go on My Big 3?

Priority 1:
_____
_____

Priority 2:
_____
_____

Priority 3:
_____
_____

Notes

Perfection is a thief.

SAM PENNY
The Topify Method

topifymethod.com

www.ingramcontent.com/pod-product-compliance
Lightning Source LLC
Chambersburg PA
CBHW070043230426
43661CB00005B/737